Old Ballynahinch

by Rose Jane Leslie, with photographs from the Gerard Sloan collection

A view of Railway Street (now known as Main Street) with the station behind the photographer, taken in 1911 when the Montalto Cycle Works was owned by a Mr Samuel Anderson. It was listed in the *Belfast Directory* as a 'Cycle and Motor Engineer' and as a stockist of petrol but by the 1940s the business had gone from the record. The Railway Hotel, first established in the 1880s as a temperance hotel, was a boarding house also offering a stopping-off point for weary cyclists who had journeyed from Belfast. In the 1950s the building changed hands to become a public house and as such is well remembered by local people. The publican, Anthony Murray, died in 1969 and today the premises is a branch of the Co-operative chemist. At the time of writing the former Montalto Cycle Works remains unused.

Text © Rose Jane Leslie, 2012.
First published in the United Kingdom, 2012,
by Stenlake Publishing Ltd.
54–58 Mill Square, Catrine,
Ayrshire, KA5 6RD.
01290 551122

www.stenlake.co.uk

ISBN 9781840335811

**The publishers regret that they cannot supply
copies of any pictures featured in this book.**

Printed by
P2D Books, 1 Newlands Rd, Westoning, Bedford, MK45 5LD

Acknowledgements

The author wishes to thank Gerard Sloan for his help in the research of this book, and also Paddy Ward and Mr and Mrs Harvey Bicker for the information and assistance they provided.

The publishers wish to thank Gerard Sloan for permission to reproduce the photographs in this book.

Further reading

Belfast and the Province of Ulster, Street Directories 1902–1969.
Bassett's Guide to County Down, 1888.
S. McCullough, *Ballynahinch – the Centre of Down*, Ballynahinch Centre of Commerce, 1968.
The Mourne Observer, *Reminiscences of Capt D.J. Bell, Ballynahinch*, 1962.
Horace Reid, *Walk about Ballynahinch*, Down County Museum, 1998.

Introduction

Ballynahinch lies in the centre of County Down at an intersection of roads leading to Belfast, Downpatrick, Newcastle, Dromore, Moira, Banbridge and Newry. The surrounding countryside is dominated by drumlins, low rounded hills formed by the melting of glaciers after the Ice Age, which are a typical feature of the county. In ancient times the drumlins were covered by heavy forest and surrounded by marshes. The name Ballynahinch derives from the Irish *Baile na hInse* for which the usual translation is 'the town of the island'. There is, of course, no island as such but a likely interpretation is that Ballynahinch was on a patch of drier land amidst the surrounding bogs.

Until the seventeenth century the Ballynahinch area was controlled by the McCartan clan. However, around 1660 their leader, Patrick McCartan, sold lands in and around Ballynahinch to Sir George Rawdon and Sir William Petty. Sir George Rawdon came from Yorkshire to Ulster in 1633 as an agent to Viscount Conway's estate near Lisburn. In addition to building up Conway's estates, Rawdon acquired property of his own and in 1681 bought an estate at Moira. Sir William Petty, who was from Hampshire, came to Ireland in 1652 and carried out a survey of the confiscated Irish lands and in the course of which produced the first accurate map of County Down. Petty leased his interest in the Ballynahinch property before his death in 1687, leaving Rawdon in sole possession. Rawdon built two corn mills and founded the original town of Ballynahinch with a market square; in 1683 Charles II granted a patent to hold a Thursday market and two fairs every February 1st and June 29th.

Towards the end of the seventeenth century settlers from lowland Scotland increased the population of the area and during the eighteenth century Ballynahinch grew as a market town where farmers could sell livestock, corn, potatoes and other crops while the cultivation of flax became increasingly significant. Around 1770 Sir John Rawdon, descendant of Sir George and created Lord Rawdon of Moira in 1750 and the Earl of Moira in 1761, moved to Ballynahinch to live at Montalto House. He improved both the estate and the town, promoted the linen market and instigated the building of the market house. He died in 1793.

In the last decade of the eighteenth century Ballynahinch was starting to prosper. Sales in the market were grossing £300 per week. Items bought and sold included yarn, linen, meat, butter, fowl, eggs, oatmeal, potatoes, shoes, wool, wool hats, horses and cattle. Elegant new townhouses, churches, a newly paved market square, shops, inns, places of entertainment and about 100 dwelling houses had appeared and by this time the town had an estimated population of 700, as recorded in Johnston's *Heterogenea*.

Unfortunately, however, the rise of the United Irishmen brought about a setback in the life of the town. Ballynahinch was one of the main battlefields in County Down in 1798 when the rebellion came to a head, which caused about the half the houses in the town to be destroyed. Montalto House was taken over as a rebel headquarters even though Lord Moira had declared to the Irish House of Lords that Ballynahinch was loyal to the Crown. In reality there was considerable support for the United Irishmen in County Down.

Not long after, in 1802, Lord Moira sold Montalto and Ballynahinch to David Ker Esq., whose family already had estates in County Antrim and at Portavo. Initially Ker did not add much to Ballynahinch, which remained in a dilapidated state in the years after the battle, apart from building corn mills in 1816 and installing pumps at the Spa wells in 1810.

The Spa wells, just over two miles outside the town, have been known since the seventeenth century for the reputed medicinal properties of their sulphurous-chalybeate waters, which were used in olden times to treat skin complaints, debility, dyspepsia and other diseases. They were situated on the Ker land at Montalto where visitors were able to sample the waters free of charge. The taking of spa waters had become a popular pastime amongst society in Bath and Cheltenham, and around the 1840 David Ker set about developing the Spa as a tourist resort along similar lines by providing pump houses and a ballroom, creating a knot garden and even building a church for the benefit of the visitors. The extension of the railway line to Ballynahinch in 1858 probably helped to improve communications for a time. Tourists continued to visit until the Second World War, though the Spa's heyday was probably over by the 1920s.

Meanwhile the population of Ballynahinch was expanding. From approximately 700 in 1800, it had risen to 911 in 1841, 1,470 in 1881, 1,500 in 1904 and to 2,816 in the 1966 census return. The 1991 census shows a population jump to 6,712, around which the number stands today. These figures and the development of new housing indicate that Ballynahinch and the nearby villages of Spa and Drumaness are convenient and popular places to live. Ballynahinch retains the identify of a market town where the Thursday market introduced during the seventeenth century still operates, even though it is much smaller in scale than it used to be.

A rank of jaunting cars, also sometimes called jarvey cars after the term used for the driver, photographed outside the railway station building in 1905, ready to convey passengers to the Spa for a fare of 6*d*. The stucco-fronted building, the work of a designer named H.H. de Wit, has since been demolished to make room for a health clinic and town library. Ballynahinch Station lay at the end of a short branch line three and a half miles off the route between Saintfield and Downpatrick on the Belfast to Newcastle line, operated by the Belfast & County Down Railway until its closure in 1950. Evidence of the old station walls is still visible near the bus terminus and nearby supermarket.

A group of drivers and others who worked at the station, photographed around 1914/15. From left, they are William Johnston, driver, with Thomas Marsh (the cart was owned by James Patterson); James Watson, James Blakely and possibly William Johnson (the cart was owned by Hugh McLeigh, proprietor of McLeigh's Hotel in the Market Square); Toal McGrillen and Samuel Glover (cart owned by McLeigh); Thomas Noade and Jim Barr, the railway clerk (cart owned by McLeigh); Barney McGrillan and John Hanna with his sons Hugh (2) and John (5) (the cart was owned by Alexander Davey); and, finally, Samuel Smyth in a car that belonged to William Poole. John Reid, who delivered parcels, stands against the building behind the carts.

In the 1920s a number of private bus companies started to operate a service between Belfast and Ballynahinch. The first of these was Harrison's, whose buses, drivers and conductors are shown here at the Belfast terminus in Cromac Square around 1926. The buses offered cheaper fares, a shorter journey distance of fifteen miles by road opposed to the 22-mile rail journey, and even the opportunity to transport farm animals. Other bus companies soon opened in competition with Harrison's, spurring a keen price war starting with a 2/6 fare to Belfast and a 2/10 return journey. Journeys could be eventful at times. Mr Harrison himself recalled sitting on a mudguard holding a cycle lamp as the only illumination one dark night coming back from Hillsborough. Eventually, the Belfast Bus Company was able to offer a fare as low as 1/- return, beating the competition between private operators, and by 1935 all the bus services were run by the Northern Ireland Transport Board.

This triumphal arch across Railway Street was one of three erected in Ballynahinch to celebrate the visit of Sir Edward Carson, MP, KC, Chairman of the Ulster Parliamentary Party, to address one of the many demonstrations which took place to express public opposition to the proposed introduction of Home Rule in Ireland. His visit took place on 28 July 1913 and, as the *Belfast Newsletter* reported, members of all the Orange lodges and Unionist clubs from miles around marched with their bands to Ednavady Hill in Montalto Demesne, home of the Earl and Countess of Clanwilliam, in a well-formed, militaristic procession. Thousands also converged from Crossgar, Downpatrick, Saintfield, Ballygowan, Comber and Belfast, having travelled by road and special trains laid on for the day. The assembled throng listened to speeches by Carson, John Miller Andrews, Lord Clanwilliam and others to affirm the view that Ulster's interests were best served by governance from London rather than Dublin. The Home Rule Bill was brought before Parliament in 1886 and 1893 when it was defeated. In 1914 it was passed but did not come into force. Finally, the 1920 Government of Ireland Act resulted in the partition of Ireland.

By 1952, when this photograph was taken, the railway line to Ballynahinch, along with all other lines south of Comber, had closed down due to the increasing popularity of road transport and the private car. The right-hand end of the station building can be seen here behind the war memorial while the former Railway Hotel premises had evidently changed hands. The war memorial currently bears the names of 50 local men who fell in the First World War and eighteen who died in the Second World War. Rising behind is Ednavady Hill, said to be the site where the rebels camped before their defeat at the Battle of Ballynahinch in 1798.

W.M. Smiley's garage and petrol pump opened around 1951 on a site at the junction of Main Street, then still Railway Street, known as Robinson's Corner. The weekly sheep market had also taken place here until about the 1940s. By 1961 Smiley's garage had been taken over by Mr Robert Caughey and was subsequently run by his sons as Caughey Bros. The business was still operating during the 1980s and the petrol pumps were finally removed some ten years ago.

The two barefooted boys seen here on the right are standing outside the Gilmore Brothers' shop while McAllister's in the right foreground, a milliner's and ladies' dress shop, displays a selection of straw boaters that would have been in fashion around 1905. This photograph was taken in 1905 from the lower end of High Street looking up the hill of Church Street. Leaning on the bicycle is a telegram boy, whose job it was to deliver telegrams around the town.

On the corner behind the trees on Market Square and the old gas lamp is McLeigh's Hotel, whose proprietor ran the jaunting car service from the station to the Spa. The hotel was built by David Ker, the town landlord, possibly in 1831. For some years it was known as Walkers Hotel before passing to the McLeighs in the early 1900s. In 1924 Hugh McLeigh, the then owner, was also a huntsman of the County Down Staghounds, and his sporting interests may explain why the hotel in that year advertised: 'To accommodate members of the coursing club special kennels have been provided for 100 dogs, and ample boarding accommodation for 100 people.' On the right the ornamented façade of the Northern Bank building of c.1860 stands out, with its 'very fine super curly aedicules and segmental pediments on the first floor, of around 1860' (as described by C.E.B. Brett in 1970). It is likely to have been the work of architects Lanyon, Lynn and Lanyon who designed a number of Northern Bank buildings at that time.

The closed shutter of the Owens family butcher premises on the left indicates that this photograph of High Street and the Market Square was taken on a Sunday morning and dates from 1920s, indicated by the 'Electricity' shop front of the office of the Electric Light and Power Company. A bus stands in Market Square, perhaps part of Johnston's Omnibus Service which went from the town on weekdays and Sundays at 8.30 a.m.

Thompson's Teas, advertised at the premises of Wallace's General Grocers in 1905. The shop is part of a row of buildings which are amongst the oldest in the town, thought to predate the Battle of Ballynahinch in 1798, after which the destruction of 61 out of 150 buildings was recorded. The extensive cellarage contained beneath them has inspired fertile local imaginations to speculate that they were used as a storage space for bodies stolen from the churchyard and traded in the name of medical research. To the right there is a good view of the Market House, which was built in 1795 by Lord Rawdon. The roof cupola subsequently disappeared until its restoration in 2002.

East Down Election, 1910.

A Meeting of the Supporters of Capt. JAMES CRAIG, the Unionist Candidate, will be held in COURTHOUSE, BALLYNAHINCH, on TUESDAY EVENING, 18th JANUARY, 1910, at 8 o'clock.

Captain JAMES CRAIG and other prominent Speakers will address the Electors.

J. ALEX. M'CONNELL, Election Agent

VOTE FOR CRAIG AND NO HOME RULE!

CRICHTON, 'RECORDER,' DOWN.

This postcard was published to publicise a meeting in Ballynahinch to address supporters of Captain James Craig, 1st Viscount Craigavon and Ulster Unionist MP for East Down from 1906–1918, issued during the 1910 election campaign. Craig achieved 4,028 votes, a majority of 974 against the Liberal candidate, one James Wood, a solicitor from Dundonald. Craig led the opposition to Home Rule and organised the Ulster Volunteers which formed the core of the Ulster Division in the First World War. He became the first Prime Minister for Northern Ireland after partition in 1922 and remained in office until he died in 1940.

One of the earliest surviving examples of a card posted in Ballynahinch, dated 12 November 1903. The house with the portico on the extreme left was the estate office of the Kers, who owned Ballynahinch and some 35,000 acres, as well as the villages of Clough, Whitehead and Ballycarry, and Downpatrick mills, schools, two ports, and quarries of slate and limestone. There was another Ker estate office in Downpatrick. On the upper floor was a hem stiching factory run by a Mrs Lemon. Other businesses on this section of the Main Street at the time were Davidson's grocer shop, spirit merchant and cycle works, Mrs Orr's confectioner, and Mooney's pub. The ghostly images of the children indicates their lack of patience in standing still long enough for the slow shutter speed of photography in those days.

Ballynahinch Market was founded in 1683 when Sir George Rawdon, then the landlord, was granted a patent by Charles II to hold a Thursday market and also two fairs on February 1st and June 29th, each to continue for three days. Permission was also granted to hold courts, which took place in the Market House built by Lord Moira (Rawdon's grandson) in 1695. As the market developed it dealt in linen, yarn, meat, butter, eggs, fowl, oatmeal, potatoes, livestock, wool and shoes. Lord Moira entertained the linen buyers at his house, Montalto, every Thursday. In the early 1900s, as this photograph shows, the market was still relatively unaltered from 100 years before. Today there is still a Thursday market in Ballynahinch though it is smaller in scale. The Market House is used for community events.

John Murdock, the 'Besom Man', sold brooms and scrubbing brushes at Ballynahinch Market from his pitch at the corner of Dromore Street and High Street all his life during the late nineteenth and early twentieth centuries. The brooms were made of heather, selected and cut by Murdock from the Dromara Hills and brought home in a donkey cart. The besoms were sold for four or five pence each, and the scrubbers for twopence. John's only rival was 'Captain' McAlea who also made brooms, carried by a cart that had one wheel larger than the other. McAlea was said to be so jealous of Murdock's success that he attacked him with his fists. The captain later suffered the unfortunate fate of being run over by the one of the first cars in the country.

This view looking towards Belfast Road shows the weekly cattle market at the turn of the twentieth century, sited on the Fair Green in front of the present war memorial. As noted in *Bassett's Directory* of 1888, 'there is no town in the county where the market produces so complete a transformation from the routine of daily life. Every street has its scene of bustling activity.' Pigs were sold on Windmill Street, explaining the old local name of Pig Street, while sheep and goats were sold on the pavement at Robinson's Corner on High Street, and horses on Dromore Street. Those selling livestock were obliged to pay a toll on entrance to the fair grounds and later a system was developed of renting out market rights.

Prior to the Second World War hiring fairs such as this one in Ballynahinch market square would have been a regular fixture in market towns in Northern Ireland. Hiring took place in May and October when young people searching for work would gather to meet farmers looking for servants or labourers. They were usually recognisable by the fact they were carrying a bundle of clothes and personal possessions. Once a hireling was chosen, the bundle would be handed over to the employer in return for a sum of money to seal the deal and they would then be taken on for a period of six months. In the photograph the hiring is taking place to the right. More men than women sought employment in this way. Mack Bros. on the right was long established as a cobbler and shoe shop and closed only in recent years.

A policeman watches the market in late afternoon some time in the late 1930s. The cart in the foreground is being loaded up, indicating that the day's trading is drawing to a close. For rural people fairs and market days provided a break from the usual daily routines and restrictions. As the day wore on a more relaxed atmosphere tended to develop; riotous behaviour and drunkenness were recorded at times. A court report of 1938 reveals that two brothers were fined 40 shillings for being drunk while in charge of a horse and cart on returning home from the market.

A view of Church Street at the junction of Dromore Street around 1924. Carville's public house can just be seen on the left and the children are congregated in front of Mrs Orr's sweet shop, beside which is Davidson's cycle works, grocer and spirit merchant, then Harrison's pub and Hamilton's shoe shop. The premises on the opposite corner with the enamel sign is Whiteside's shop and to the right can be seen the rails round the town pump, frequently referred to as 'Whiteside's Pump' by local people.

Ednavady Hill lies behind Dromore Street in this 1904 view out of the town. As the handwritten note on the postcard states, 'the fighting was thickest in the Battle of Ballynahinch in 1798, when Betsy Gray was the Irish "Joan of Arc"'. Ballynahinch was the scene of one of the fiercest battles of the 1798 rebellion and Betsy Gray was a nineteen year old girl who insisted upon accompanying her sweetheart and her brother to the battlefield. On the way home after the battle she was shot dead by a one of a group of Hillsborough yeoman, a tragedy which has implanted her name in folk memory. Dromore Street was the site of the grain market; on the left there is a grain store with louvred windows and a roof chute.

Dromore Street again, but looking towards the town centre. The railings of the town pump are gone, dating the picture to sometime after 1932 when mains water was introduced. Weirs Cattle Feeds is on the left where sacks are piled on the pavement. The original linen hall once stood on the right, also near the site of the original Catholic chapel. Before the chapel was built the site was a 'mass station' where Roman Catholics worshipped in the open air in the years when public celebration of mass services was prohibited until the Act of Catholic Emancipation was passed in 1829.

The number of assembled farm carts, motor vehicles and people suggest this scene of Dromore Street was taken on a market day in the 1930s. Gourley's Boot Merchant and Shoe Shop in the foreground lasted until the 1990s. A bread van is parked outside John Bell's grocer's shop, which was next door to Leahy's pub. Other businesses on Dromore Street at that time included Joseph Sloan the tailor, Francis Russell veterinary surgeon, Boyd's pub, Richard Carville car driver, J.A. Charles hardware and grocers, Joseph Whan the shoemaker, and Joseph McGibney blacksmith.

The films advertised at the old picture house are *Hell Divers*, *Smilin' Through*, *Flying High*, all released in 1931, and *Hold Your Man* from 1933. The cinema continued until the 1960s when a ticket cost 9d. Today, the entrance of the cinema building has been altered and it now houses the Free Presbyterian Church which opened in 1968. The Orange Hall adjacent is much the same apart from a simplification of the window panes above the entrance. A commemorative plaque shows that it was opened on 27 December 1932 by Lord Gilford, whose family seat of Montalto has its front gates almost opposite the hall. The foundation stone was laid by the Right Honourable J.M. Andrews DL MP, on 17 October 1931 and the building is still used for its original intended purpose.

In June 1914, Lord Gilford, son of the Earl of Clanwilliam, was born. As part of the celebrations for the arrival of the son and heir, the Ballynahinch Company of the Ulster Volunteer Force erected this banner above the front gates of Montalto House. The East Down UVF was raised by Lord Clanwilliam, and the local company had spent time training at Montalto estate, billeted in the farmyard. A big reception awaited, consisting of guests with the entire company and the band. As recalled by Captain W.D. Bell, who was in charge, the event was, 'our last social occasion before we joined up'. This was with the Ulster Division which incurred such heavy losses at the Battle of the Somme.

By 1912, the date of this photograph, Montalto House belonged to the Earl and Countess of Clanwilliam. They had bought the property from David Ker in 1910, having moved from their ancestral home of Gill Hall at Dromore because, the story goes, Lady Clanwilliam disliked that it was haunted. The Earl of Clanwilliam was descended from Sir John Meade who was created Baronet of Ireland in 1703. Another Sir John Meade was made an Irish Earl of Clanwilliam in 1766. Montalto was built originally by the Earl of Moira in the 1780s and David Ker bought the house in 1802. His son, also David, added another storey to the house, as well as a ballroom and servant wing. The Clanwilliams demolished the service wing and sold Montalto in 1979. Today the house is an exclusive private hotel.

In 1881 Captain Richard Ker established the County Down Staghounds which hunted red deer. There were kennels for the hounds at Montalto and deer were also kept on the property. As noted in the 1888 *Bassett's County Down Directory*, the pack had 120 members. Hunting took place three times a week and members paid an annual subscription of ten guineas with an annual dinner taking place in Belfast. In 1910, when Captain Ker was still in charge, the hunt had 34 couples of hounds and there were 52 deer in the herd. In 1968 the Staghounds had 25 full members and 25 subscribing, one third of whom were female, with hunts twice weekly during the season from 1 November to 1 April. It is still functioning today as the Down Hunt.

Charlie McGee drove a jaunting car between Ballynahinch Railway Station and the Spa for many years. He is pictured here in front of the Assembly Rooms at the Spa, which were built in 1840 by David Ker as a meeting point for the visitors. It was described at the time as 'a newsroom with a ballroom over, and an attached room for mufflings etc.' Dances and concerts were held in the ballroom until the 1950s. The Spa wells were on the Montalto estate and were used by the visitors free of charge. A knot garden known as a puzzle walk was also created for the benefit of the visitors. The Assembly Rooms are now in possession of the Masonic order and the upstairs ballroom retains its wooden sprung floor and floor length mirrors but the Rooms' original wooden porch with Doric columns has disappeared.

Mary Jane Palmer, along with her sister Anne, was employed to look after the pumps at the Spa wells some time before 1894 when a Matthew Bell was listed in *Slater's Directory* as the keeper of the Baths and Pump Room. The pumps, made by Bramah in London, were installed by David Ker in 1810 and hip baths were later made available for those wishing to get into the water. The Spa was visited mainly in summer, from the middle of May to the end of September. As explained by Dr Alexander Knox in *Irish Watering Places* (1845), this was when the waters were believed to be at their greatest strength and purity, being undiluted by the rains of winter. Today, the pumps belong to the Masonic order and are still preserved for safekeeping nearby.

The Assembly Rooms in the 1930s, by then owned and run by a Mrs Flinn and known as the Spa Roadhouse. During the Second World War the building was occupied by soldiers. The Assembly Rooms now contain a beautician's premises although the days when they were used for dances and concerts are still remembered by local people.

The Spa Golf Club was formed in 1907 by the owner of the Elmwood Hotel in the background, a Mrs H. Isaac. Advertisements of the day proclaimed the hotel, 'The Wiesbaden of the North'. By the 1920s the proprietor was Mrs W.R. Flinn and it was advertised at that time as, 'one of the finest hotels in the North of Ireland. Exquisite new tennis and croquet lawns, Sulphur and Iron springs, Hot Sulphur Baths, large comfortable rooms, late dinner. Adjoining Golf Links.' Today, the golf links are built over and the former Elmwood Hotel, which has been extended, rendered and painted white, is a nursing home.

ECHO HALL, SPA, BALLYNAHINCH, CO. DOWN.

Echo Hall, near the Spa, appears to date from the late eighteenth century. A map of 1791 indicates that the house was part of the Montalto estate and its relatively modest size, originally five bays across, suggests Echo Hall was an agent or steward's house. It is said that supporters of the United Irishmen stayed there before the Battle of Ballynahinch in 1798. This photograph, dating from 1906, shows Mr John Cooper whose family had a drapery business in High Street, Ballynahinch. It was listed in *Bassett's Directory* of 1888 as 'John Cooper, Wholesale and Retail Draper' and continued until the 1900s. From about 1912 until the 1950s Echo Hall was a boarding house and the house then passed to the ownership of a Mr and Mrs Johnstone, changing hands again in 1976 to Mr and Mrs Bicker, the present owners.

Drumaness village, some three and three-quarter miles south of Ballynahinch, developed along the River Comber and was centred on the spinning mill which was built in 1850 by John Davidson and Thomas Chermside of Belfast. In 1858 the mill was sold to James Lamont Brown and his partner Charles Hurst. Flax yarn, which latterly supplied the Ulster Weaving Company, continued in production until the mill closed in 1968, when it still belonged to the Hurst family. Today the mill is demolished and the lake in the centre of this view has been drained. The mill workers' houses, some of which are listed, are still preserved and Drumaness village remains a thriving community which the 2001 census recorded as having over 1,200 inhabitants. Flax is the crop growing in the foreground of this photograph by Thomas Gribben.

Drumaness village in the early 1900s showing the Dan Rice Memorial Hall with clock tower, with the schoolhouse (built in 1850) on the left and the mill in the background. The gentleman in the peaked cap is Mr Hurst, the mill owner. At the time of the photograph the hall contained a dining room, reading room and billiard room, all provided for the mill workers. It was renamed in the 1970s after Dan Rice, a Nationalist councillor who represented Drumaness during the 1950s and 60s, and is today a thriving community centre run by the council. There is still a primary school in the village though no longer in the old schoolhouse building.

The owners of Drumaness Mill encouraged their workers to play sport, offering sponsorship and pitches to play on. This photograph of Drumaness Cricket Team, showing the mill buildings in the background, was taken around 1941/42. In the back row, from left, are Patrick Rogan, Patrick McCabe, Bob Lennon, William Nixon, Eddie Boyd and Bob Reid. The younger boy, aged about ten, is Alphonsus Rogan, son of Patrick. In the front row are Jim Strain, Bob Johnston, Tom Lewis, Bert Lennon, Willie Strain and John Boyd. It is likely that the cups were prizes in local competitions such as the Trades League in nearby Downpatrick. Today, Drumaness Cricket Team is a member of the Northern Cricket Union Senior League, Section Two.

Originally known as Tir na Og 'Young Ireland' Gaelic football club, now Drumaness GAA, this club was founded in 1935. In the early days the members practised on a field on Comber Road belonging to the McCaughertys until the 'Paradise Park' playing field was acquired by the club around 1945/46. The photograph was taken when the team won the Junior League in 1946/47. The members are, back row, left to right: Herbie Noade, Gerry McNamara, D. Madine, J. Peake, Patsy McMullan; middle row: Ted Nixon, Seamus McMullan, H. Rogers, J. Magee; front row: H. Marner. D. Bell, P. McCreanor, C. McCartan, Jimmy McGivern.

Harris's Mill at the outskirts of Ballynahinch on the Newcastle Road was built by David Ker in 1816. As noted in the *Ordnance Survey Memoirs* of the 1830s the mill 'works five months on an average, water supplied by Ballynahinch River in sufficient quantity. Nature of water wheel in breast diameter of water wheel 17 and a half feet, breadth of water wheel 5 feet, diameter of cog wheel 8 feet.' Ker later built a scutch mill where the flax could be separated by the adjoining corn mill. Throughout the twentieth century the mill was still used. At the beginning of the Second World War 30 men and women worked there but by 1950s the workforce consisted of just two men. Around 1958 Harris's Mill ceased to scutch flax, finishing with an order for the firm of Andrews of Comber, but the mill remains in working order and is still used occasionally.

Construction of the St Patrick's Roman Catholic Church in Ballynahinch started in 1807 on a site given by Mr David Ker in exchange for the site of the first chapel on the old linen hall which is now the fire station in Dromore Street. Lack of funds meant that the church was still not complete by 1812. However, in June that year the *Belfast Newsletter* published a notice: 'A sermon will be preached in Ballynahinch on Sunday, 5th July by Rev. Mr Curran, of Downpatrick, for the benefit of the New Chapel as yet unfinished, from the inability of the congregation. It is to be hoped that the liberal of all denominations will contribute their units for the above purpose.' The resulting funds enabled its completion soon after but destruction caused by a catastrophic storm in January 1839 necessitated extensive repairs. The church was rededicated in 1843 and further alterations were made in 1866 when transepts and a tower designed by W.J. Barre of Belfast were added.

A first communion service taking place at a field in the hilly land at Dunmore about four miles south of Ballynahinch, not far from the Spa. In the background the pathways worn into the ground indicate their use by worshippers over a long period, suggesting that this scene is at the site of a Penal Mass station at Guiness. The town land of Dunmore is served by St Colman's Church, a centre of Catholic worship from ancient times, historical information that was recalled by the Rev B.J. Mooney. This photograph was taken by local photographer Thomas Gribben (1882–1959) in 1920.

Ballynahinch Congregational Church was formed in 1902 by Presbyterians who were no longer prepared to worship in any of Ballynahinch's three churches as all their ministers were supporters of Home Rule. This church, which collapsed under heavy snowfall on 28 December 1908, smashing all the contents except the organ and a few chairs, was a temporary structure built of corrugated iron on the Dromore Road, on Ker family land. Plans for a permanent building, already underway, had to be accelerated and the new brick structure opened in July 1910, sited almost opposite where the iron church had stood. In the intervening period Richard Ker permitted the congregation to use the Market House.

Ballymaglave LOL 568 from the Ballynahinch area marching on High Street sometime between 1902 and 1904. The lodge is accompanied by two Lambeg drummers and a fife player in the manner customary at that time, before the formation of the many bands that are seen on 12 July parades today. Then as now, however, Lambeg drums are still played in Ballynahinch on Orangeman's Day. The parade is passing Walker's Medical Hall, which remains a chemist's shop, in this postcard by R.B. Bailie of Ballynahinch, a watchmaker, jeweller, general merchant and shipping agent.

St Joseph's Ardtanagh Pipe Band, photographed in the 1930s; kneeling in the centre of the front row is Frank Rainey, holding bagpipes bought by his father from Robert Lawrie of Glasgow, a renowned pipe maker, using savings of £5. His descendants recall that the original intention was to spend all the money on high quality pipes with ivory parts but, in the event, Mr Rainey spent only 2s 10d on a less expensive instrument. The band is thought to have formed around 1900 as a flute band attached to the Ancient Order of the Hibernians in the Ardtanagh townland, near Loughinisland. Other members identifiable include Hugh Maguire, second from left in the front row, also Leo and John Rogan to the right of Frank Rainey. In the back row Johnnie Rogan is second from left, beside him is possibly Tom McAleenan, then Willie Carvill, with John Gelston at the end of the row. Over the years the band has shed its links with the Ancient Order of the Hibernians and reformed several times, with its most recent disbandment in 2006. It achieved Grade 4 in the Royal Scottish Pipe Band association, winning first place in 2005.

Mourneview and Fair Green looking towards the Belfast Road as it was in the 1950s or 60s, with the Assumption Grammar School for girls in the background. The Assumption was a religious congregation formed in Paris in the 1880s. In the early twentieth century a daughter congregation in South Africa was led by Mother Baptist McKenny who came from Ballygowan; in 1932 she formed a community in Ballynahinch. In September 1933 the Assumption High School opened with 20 boarders. After the 1947 Education Act it became the Assumption Grammar School and over the years the enrolment gradually increased from 250 in 1960 to 695 in 1982 and 910 in 2000, around which figure it stands today. The convent was incorporated into the school and a new convent was built elsewhere in 2004.

The pupils of St Patrick's Boys Primary with their schoolmaster, Mr Nangle, photographed in 1920/21 at the former school in Railway Street, which was demolished in 1958. The Roman Catholic school was established in 1864 with two classrooms, one for boys, the other for girls. A majority of the boys here can be named as follows. *Front row, from left*: A. McAlister, ? Flynn, G. Irvine, K. Irvine, H.W. Owens, M. McCauley, J. Hanvey, R. Murray. *Second row*: J. Walker, T. McGrillen, ? Lew, J. McKelvey, M. Walker, P. McGuigan, ? Flynn, G. McCauley, T. Duffield, P. Kane, J. Drake, W. Madine, N. McGrillen, A. Moore, J. Duffield. *Third row*: W. Carville, T. Madine, B. Madine, E. McGuiggan, J. Owens, D. Kerr, J. Colgan, H. Woade, J. Hanvey, J. Branney, H.F. Duffy, G. Mullan, A. Davey, T. Duffield, T. Murray. *Fourth row*: James Fitzpatrick, H. McGurnaghan, J. Rice, H. Madine, P. Smyth, A. Rice, D. McGrillen, J. Murray, B. McAllister, T. Rush, S. Flynn, R. Milligan, unknown, A. Hanna. *Back row*: T. Toman, ? Hanvey, F. Hanna, J. Hanna, William Sloan, H. Owens, H. McGrath, J. Mullan, T. Mullan, Thomas McKeown, H. Woade, Desmond McGrath, W. Watson, J. Madine.

The Irish football team at Windsor Park in 1913 after their first victory over the England team, when the *Ireland's Saturday Night* newspaper presented medals to all the team members. Seated in the front row of players on the right is Frank Thompson, the 5'7" 'Ballynahinch Bantam' and celebrated left winger, born in Railway Street, Ballynahinch, in 1885. Thompson's achievements included 12 full caps for Ireland from 1910–1914, scoring two goals. He played for Cliftonville, Irish cup winners in 1908/09 and Irish league winners in 1909/10 and next for Linfield, winners of the Irish league in 1910/11. In April 1910 he went to Bradford City. The team won the FA Cup in 1911 against Newcastle United, and all eleven team members received a medal. In 2003 Thompson's FA Cup medal sold at auction for £23,000. In 1913 he joined the Scottish First Division side Clyde, an association that lasted 21 years, first as a player then as manager. Thompson died in 1950.

A housekeeper looks out of the front door of Dr Brown's house, now a coffee shop, along Railway Street from the town centre end in the 1920s. Through the archway doors there would have been a yard, stabling and outbuildings for the family pony and trap. Douglas Funeral Directors, two doors along opened in 1926 and is still in business. Railway Street, now Main Street, is the widest street in the town and was first mapped in the Ordnance Survey of the 1830s when a coach service to Belfast was also established.

At 300 feet above sea level, the highest point on the Belfast & County Down Railway, Ballynahinch Station was at the end of a short branch line off the main railway line between Comber and Downpatrick. It opened in 1858 but there was immediate competition from omnibus proprietors and carriers, who all had to be bought out. Seen here in July 1936, a six-wheeled bread van is in the foreground and a diesel engine is on the right. When the station was designed it was envisaged as part of a through route to Banbridge to connect with the Belfast to Dublin line, a plan never carried out.

This Harland and Wolff diesel electric engine 2-4-0 standing at Ballynahinch Station was hired by the Belfast & County Down Railway in 1933 as an economy measure for use on the Ballynahinch branch, where, as a small tributary carrying relatively few passengers, the older and lesser trains were relegated. This train continued in use until the line closed in 1950, when it was returned to the manufacturer. It was painted dark green and was apparently never repainted during its use on the line.

Ballynahinch Junction Station was about four miles from town, and was where passengers changed to the Belfast to Newcastle line. This photograph, taken during the 1930s, is from the footbridge where the train towards Newcastle is on the right while on the left the engine has been detached from the carriages, before completing the process of reversing along the track in order to take the train back to Ballynahinch. The water tower, which dates from 1857, was operated first by a steam pump and later by wind power. Like Ballynahinch Station, this station was in operation between 10 September 1858 and 16 January 1950.

This windmill, on a hill overlooking the town, was built in 1773 by Lord Moira to grind corn grown locally. It was soon realised that water-powered mills were a more efficient than windmills, which had sails that were easily damaged. The sails assumed a more gruesome aspect when Hugh McCullough, Colonel of the Bangor United Irishmen was hanged from them following his capture as he retreated after the Battle of Ballynahinch in 1798. In recent times the windmill tower has been restored, surrounded by grounds accessible to the public.